Also by Libby McGugan

The Eidolon

The Fifth Force

The Game Changer

THE POWER
OF THE
LEMON

LIBBY MCGUGAN

BALBOA.PRESS
A DIVISION OF HAY HOUSE

Balboa Press books may be ordered through booksellers or by contacting:

Balboa Press
A Division of Hay House
1663 Liberty Drive
Bloomington, IN 47403
www.balboapress.co.uk
UK TFN: 0800 0148647 (Toll Free inside the UK)
UK Local: (02) 0369 56325 (+44 20 3695 6325 from outside the UK)

Because of the dynamic nature of the Internet, any web addresses or
links contained in this book may have changed since publication and
may no longer be valid. The views expressed in this work are solely those
of the author and do not necessarily reflect the views of the publisher,
and the publisher hereby disclaims any responsibility for them.

The author of this book does not dispense medical advice or prescribe
the use of any technique as a form of treatment for physical, emotional,
or medical problems without the advice of a physician, either directly
or indirectly. The intent of the author is only to offer information
of a general nature to help you in your quest for emotional and
spiritual well-being. In the event you use any of the information in
this book for yourself, which is your constitutional right, the author
and the publisher assume no responsibility for your actions.

Any people depicted in stock imagery provided by Getty Images are
models, and such images are being used for illustrative purposes only.
Certain stock imagery © Getty Images.

Cover art: ©hebrideansnapper

Print information available on the last page.

ISBN: 978-1-9822-8672-9 (sc)
ISBN: 978-1-9822-8673-6 (e)

Balboa Press rev. date: 12/01/2022

For Graham, who lives his Light

YOU ARE NOT JUST THE DROP
IN THE OCEAN.
YOU ARE THE MIGHTY OCEAN
IN THE DROP.

RUMI

CONTENTS

FOREWORD

Libby's book is a love song that will remind you of the beauty and vastness that you are! And like a favourite song, it is meant to be listened to and be moved by, over and over again. Allow the wisdom of this song to resonate with your soul, the loving essence of who you truly are.

Listen to this song without thinking, from an open heart. Don't focus on Libby's words but to where she is pointing. Freely explore this space within. Revel in the silence you find beyond the words, and fill with the radiant feeling that reveals itself from there. Peaceful silence and a loving feeling, these are the gifts given to all who surrender into this space within. And as Libby advises, when resting in your heart, trust wherever it moves you.

This little book is a profound reminder of your inner heart and wisdom, your innate well-being. Libby is pointing you to your true home, your true Self. May the beauty of her song uplift and liberate you as you allow love and wisdom to dance you through life.

I am so grateful to Libby for writing this book! I know I will pass it on to many, and I just know you will want to share this with family and friends. Enjoy!

Dicken Bettinger, Ed.D.
Licensed psychologist, retired
3 Principles Practitioner and Trainer
Co-author of Coming Home: Uncovering the Foundations of Psychological Well-being

PREFACE

This book is a collection of insights that dropped in along the way; fleeting glimpses of the mystery of Life and the subtle miracle we live within.

Some of these insights came from other people, some I figured out but mostly it feels like I'm simply the vessel *through* which they land… the lightning rod that channels the current onto the page.

It's laid out to take you from the comfort of your personal thinking, where most of us live these days, into your expanded broader being – the intelligence of your body, the wisdom of your heart and the light of your soul.

You can read it cover to cover or dip in and out. Sometimes flipping open a book to a seemingly 'random' page gives you what you need most in that moment.

A mixture of soul musings and down-to-earth ramblings, my hope is that it helps point you towards a deeper awareness of who you really are, towards your own wisdom and light which is always, eternally within you, and to remind you just how supported and loved you are by Life.

With love,

Libby

ACKNOWLEDGMENTS

To Graham, who lives this guidance naturally, thank you for your unwavering love, wisdom, strength and support, for your creative lifeforce, for always being up for adventure and for being my rock. And thank you for your beautiful cover art for this book.

To my teacher Dicken Bettinger, thank you for your inspiring example of living in presence, for your strong steady guidance, your clear, simple message of the power of love and your light-hearted awe of Life.

To Kate McCavana, thank you for your joyful curiosity, the magic you bring to life, your pointing towards the wealth of spirit, and your gentle wise counsel in business and play.

To Lubna Kerr and Lex Farndell, thank you for your love, patience, friendship, counsel and creative daring through the thoughtstorms and the sunshine.

To Sandy Powel, May Arado, Donald Stephens and all the team at Balboa Press, whose kind assistance and attention to detail brought this book into being and helped share it with others, thank you for all that you do to bring more light into the world.

To all the teachers I've learned from, and continue to learn from along the way, thank you for helping me wake up to the magnificence of reality and the part we play in it all. In particular to Sydney Banks, Wayne Dyer, Abraham Hicks, Kyle Cease, Eckhart Tolle, Nassim Haramein, Vishen Lakhiani, Bentinho Massaro, Mooji, Helen Hadsell, Gabrielle Bernstein, Joe Dispenza, Matt Kahn and Joseph Campbell.

And to you, thank you for taking the time to read this book and look in this direction.

INTRODUCTION

Imagine you're in your kitchen. On a wooden chopping board in front of you is a large, plump yellow lemon. Take a knife and cut it carefully into quarters, see the juice spill out onto the wood, breathe in its sharp citrussy scent. Lift one of the lemon segments to your mouth, feel the fleshy capsules bursting with liquid as it touches your lips. Now, take a bite. What happens?

If you're like most people, your cheeks pucker, your saliva glands cave in and your mouth waters like a running tap. You might shiver or wince. Your body has an immediate, visceral and very real response to... what? A lemon?

No. To a *thought about a lemon*.

The power of the lemon is that it shows us the power of thought. This is the doorway to our inner power.

The lemon is one of our greatest teachers. Not only does it illustrate in real, physical terms that we are experiencing our thoughts, it also points us to the power of our creativity in shaping our reality. There is no lemon. Simply the act of *focusing on a thought about a lemon*, shapes our experience in that moment and our body responds immediately, *as if the lemon was real.*

Do you see the power of Thought?

CHAPTER ONE

MIND

Our minds are miraculous...

Creating stories,

Pondering pasts,

Imagining futures.

A single viewpoint in Infinity's wisdom.

Like a child needs a parent

To hold her hand steady,

Our mind needs our presence

To align with our soul.

LIBBY MCGUGAN

Beyond the noise of our personal mind's chatter is an unchanging stillness. When all thinking falls away, there remains a space of wisdom, where the answer to any problem is found. This space is presence.

~ Notice how it feels when your personal thinking settles down.

Let your mind breathe

In its own time

Breathe in fresh thoughts,

Fresh ideas, fresh insights.

Breathe out

Who you no longer are.

Like a wave on the ocean, our state of mind peaks
and troughs over time. When we stop trying to
manage it, our natural intelligence brings our
mind back to healthy balance. From this place
of spacious presence, higher quality thoughts
occur to us – we don't have to figure things out.

**~ Let go of your grip on addictive thinking
and notice fresh thoughts showing up.**

Our mind has its own rhythm,

Its own intelligence.

It knows how to clear itself.

To see through a glass of sandy water,

Put it down, let it be.

The sand settles in its own time,

The water clears.

So it is with thoughts in our mind.

LIBBY MCGUGAN

Have you noticed that your best ideas occur to you when you're doing something else, like having a shower or driving? Left to themselves, thoughts settle down and our mind clears on its own, making space for new thought.

~ Keep a light touch.
There's no need to interfere.

As the waves rise and fall

And the sun rises and sets,

Nature's rhythm ebbs and flows

In your mind.

There is a time for everything.

Wait until daylight

To see your next step.

LIBBY MCGUGAN

We're part of something far bigger that knows the right timing for everyone and everything. As frustrating as it can be to feel stuck, there is a perfect time for things to change and it may not be right now. That's okay. When they do, it will be just right.

~ Trust that things will change when they're ready to.

The river of thought

Is always flowing,

Bringing fresh ideas

To drink.

All it needs

Is for you to look up

From old thoughts

And welcome the new.

The answer to any problem already exists. We just can't see it when we're tuned to the *thought about the problem.* The power of letting go of thought is that it creates space for new thoughtforms – new solutions – to come into our awareness. It's easy to recognise them – they come with a feeling of peace, common sense and rightness.

~ What new thoughtforms bubble up when you let go of old thinking?

Being caught in an eddy of thinking,

It's okay.

Relax,

Let go.

Trust will carry you

To calm waters.

One of the rules of swimming is that when you get caught underwater, don't fight the current. You can't win. So it is with overthinking – when you let go and trust, you'll naturally and effortlessly open up into the spaciousness of peace. From here, you'll feel better and you'll know what to do.

~ Let go.

It's okay not to know

When you know Life knows.

LIBBY MCGUGAN

It's funny how often we forget that we can't know everything. Life would be dull if we did. No surprises, no adventures. What we do know is an infinitesimal drop in the ocean of what there is to know. All we really need to know is that there is a solution and it will show up in the right way at the right time. We don't have to worry about it.

~ What will you do with all your spare time when you stop worrying?

Thoughtstorms come and go

The sky doesn't mind.

The sun always shines

Behind the clouds.

You are not your thoughts,

You are the sky,

Always illuminated by the sun.

Realising you are not your thoughts is a gamechanger. As believable as they may seem, thoughts are only suggestions. You don't have to buy into them. You are the one *observing* thoughts... the one who chooses which thoughts to focus on. This is the seat of your power.

~ What happens when you become the observer of your thoughts?

The quieter the dawn,

The more you hear the birdsong.

The quieter your mind,

The more you hear your soulsong.

LIBBY MCGUGAN

Who you really are is before your thoughts.

When you get quiet and listen, you'll

begin to hear it and feel it – your unique

vibration that no-one else can be.

~ Get curious about, and familiar

with, the real you.

The Little Mind thinks it knows.

The Big Mind smiles.

Our egos are like protective shells, keeping us safe from what we don't understand. Innocently, they make things up to justify our position and we believe them, so we stay small. Watch what your mind tells you when you feel afraid. Is it *really* true? Our egos keep us safe until we are ready to expand. Once you see this, you'll want to crack open that shell and grow beyond it. That's when you shift from surviving to thriving and begin to live.

~ What thoughts are keeping you small?

Look beyond the walls of intellect,

Of what you think you know,

To the infinite space of wisdom,

To what you don't know yet.

Through her gentle guidance,

Your best life unfolds

And you realise

The whole Universe is on your side.

There is so much more to discover beyond our old assumptions. Imagine the freedom of living your best life, unencumbered by doubt. *How* it happens is the adventure you're here to live.

~ Are you ready to step into your best life?

Thoughtforms are the paint

That colour your world.

Your focus is the brush.

The world is your canvas.

You are the artist.

The world is made of thought – it colours our experience in every moment. We're painting scenes through our attention to thoughtforms, literally creating new worlds. Take back your power – paint scenes you want to see rather than settling for someone else's artwork.

~ What life do you want to paint today?

Attention is your superpower.

What you give your attention to

Comes to life.

We think we're observing the world. We're not – we're creating it. Whether we create the same things day in, day out, is up to us. When we realise we are creating in every moment, we can use our superpower for good.

~ Begin to shift your focus towards what you would prefer to experience for yourself and others and watch what happens.

CHAPTER TWO

BODY

Your miraculous body,

With more cells than there are stars in our galaxy...

Each their own universe

Dancing for a lifetime

In perfect timing,

With the symphony that is you.

How often do we appreciate the miracle of
our body, a perfect vessel for us to explore
and engage with life? It asks very little from
us – water, rest, exercise, a healthy diet and
healthy thoughts – in return it gives us a
home. Remember the power of the lemon?
Our cells are listening and responding.

~ What thoughts are you feeding your body?

We don't know how to digest food

Or heal cuts

Or turn light into a lover's eyes…

A deeper intelligence

Takes care of it all.

All we need do

Is love and intend.

The fact that you're reading this is a miracle.
Billions of processes are taking place effortlessly
and naturally simply because you intended to
read what's on this page. A natural intelligence
is coordinating everything for you.

~ Can you see how powerful your intention is?

Listen to your body

It will tell you in each moment

Where your focus lies...

Tension is tuning to the mind's anxious illusions.

Ease is tuning to the soul's peaceful truth.

LIBBY MCGUGAN

We are in constant dialogue with our body. Our mind speaks in thoughts and our body speaks in feelings. It helps to become bilingual – tune to the subtle language of how your body feels. It will tell you everything you need to know before you embark on a train of thought. The most helpful question is: *how does this thought make me feel?*

**~ Remember your power to
choose what you focus on.
If you don't like the feeling of a
thought, back up and let go.
A new one will be along any moment.**

Like putting your hand on a hot stove

Is meant to hurt,

Tension is the signal

To drop all thinking

And fall into presence.

All feelings are helpful, especially the uncomfortable ones. We have a simple, reliable and effective biofeedback system within us that helps us navigate our thinking and shape our experience.

~ How would your experience change if you saw feelings as friendly indicators?

Like a tuning fork resonates

With its true frequency,

Your body resonates

With what is true for you.

Leave your mind out of it.

Trust your resonance.

LIBBY MCGUGAN

You know when something feels true for you.
It may not make sense to your rational mind,
but if it resonates with you, it's your truth. You
feel your body light up – maybe a ripple along
your spine or beneath your skin. Your mind may
try to talk you out of it, but your resonance
will tell you what's true. Like you know when
you love someone, truth needs no explaining,
justifying or defending. You just know.

~ What truth is your body telling you?

Like rivers wash through soil,

Feelings wash through your body.

Let the good ones inspire dreams.

Let the bad ones pass...

The thoughts they carry

Are not for you.

Shift your gaze to the space of dreams

And choose again.

We are constantly being offered choices in shaping our experience. We're more like open vessels than solid beings – a channel for all kinds of thoughts and feelings. Life trusts us enough to choose. With a bit of practice, it becomes fun to decide what we focus on and watch what happens.

~ Give it a go and play with your power to shape things for good today.

Do you know where your feelings come from?

Not people, not circumstances, not the world.

They come from the thoughts you're focusing on.

Feelings are friendly indicators

Helping us tune our focus,

Guiding us to create our best lives.

Understanding that feelings are indicators is the shortcut to a peaceful and creative life. When you think a happy thought, you feel happy. When you think a miserable thought, you feel miserable. Life is easier when you make friends with feelings and let them guide your point of focus.

~ What could you create if you let your feelings be the compass for your thoughts?

Beauty is here

In every moment.

Soften your gaze,

Quiet the noise

And you'll see it

And hear it

And feel it

And be it.

Try walking down the street listening

to your favourite soundtrack.

~ What beauty do you see that

you never noticed before?

How beautiful

That we are all different.

Each snowflake unique and perfect,

Yet all are made of water.

We're all powered by the same lifeforce. We're all one in essence, each with our own unique expression. Comparison with others makes no sense when you realise that only you can be you and you're meant to be you for a reason.

~ What beauty do you see in yourself today?

I am you

You are me.

The same breath

Breathes us.

The same love

Lives us.

LIBBY MCGUGAN

We like to think we're separate and that we belong to our own tribe. We like to think we're looking in on nature, studying it, observing it, prodding at it, but we can't escape the truth that we are all part of a beautiful, natural, unified system. We are all breathed by the same air and lived by the same lifeforce. We are one.

~ What happens when you see other people as another part of you?

Love is intelligent.

It knows what to do.

Trust it.

LIBBY MCGUGAN

Love is the fabric of everything, including your body. It is the space within and between all things. It's not an empty space – it's alive with the energy of creation. It forms things out of nothing. It is infinitely intelligent.

~ Tune to the space within you and watch what happens.

Celebrate your body...

Its beautiful intelligence,

The exquisite orchestration

Of trillions of cells,

Each with the intention of you thriving.

It asks for very little

Yet offers a lifelong home.

Honour this gift.

Enjoy it every day.

~ How lucky we are to be alive here and now.

Children thrive with love.

Friendships blossom with kindness.

Flowers bloom with appreciation.

Nurture your body in the same way,

With kindness, appreciation and love.

LIBBY MCGUGAN

Your body loves to be appreciated. The energy of appreciation is like a spa for your cells. They relax and function at their best health when we allow this energy to flow.

~ Take your cells to the spa every day and show them some love.

CHAPTER THREE

HEART

Our heart is the awareness

Of the miracle of love.

Love is the most powerful force in the Universe. It is the fabric of Life and the energy that connects all living things.

**~ Notice what happens when
you open your heart
to the love that is within you
and around you today.**

When you're light-hearted,

You're on track.

LIBBY MCGUGAN

Light has been used as a metaphor for millennia to describe our true nature... 'light-hearted', 'light up', 'enlightened'. Keep it simple – life is meant to feel good and when we're tuned to light, we're tuned to love.

~ 'Let go of what feels heavy and move towards what feels light.'

~ Kyle Cease

Hearts are made to connect.

Let your mind fall silent.

Just being is enough.

True connection happens when we fall out of
our personal thinking and become present
with another. Without the judgements and
complications of mind-games, our hearts
recognise ourselves in others. This is compassion.

~ How does it feel to truly

connect with another?

"Everyone is doing the best they can given the thinking they have that looks real to them."

~ Sydney Banks.

Our heart-space holds no judgement, only love. When we're in our heart-space, there are no conditions. Look beyond any thinking and see people as they really are. It might surprise you to realise what you're looking at.

~ Try seeing someone from this place of no judgement today.

Trees whisper to each other

On the breeze.

Listen to your heart's wordless whisperings.

It knows your dreams.

Let it lead you.

Our heart knows our deepest desires and sometimes our mind tries to talk us out of them. How often do we shut ourselves off from our best life because we don't take the time to listen, or we choose to play small?

~ *'Let your mind live inside your heart.'*
~ *Mooji*

Love, compassion, kindness

Are the fabric of you.

They are omnipresent

When judgement dissolves.

We don't have to try to be compassionate or kind or loving. It's our natural state when we let go of old assumptions. The more present we are, the more connected we are. Presence is the space between and within everyone and everything – there's nowhere that it's not, including within you.

~ How does it feel to be compassionate towards yourself?

Listen

With no thought

Of what you might say in return.

Just listen.

Your presence is love.

LIBBY MCGUGAN

Your presence is the greatest gift you can give another. Drop out of your mind into your heart and listen from here, with no agenda.

~ Listen to the energy connecting both of you and watch what happens.

True love

Needs no words.

LIBBY MCGUGAN

We spend so much time talking, texting, emailing, messaging. Words, words, words… always trying to explain, to justify, to prove something right. True love stops us in our tracks. Perhaps for the first time, we drop the words and let ourselves feel. A whole new wordless world opens up when we do.

~ What happens when you fall silent and feel?

As the sun blazes

Over the sleeping ocean,

Our hearts ignite

In the joy of love.

Dispelling illusion,

Radiating truth.

LIBBY MCGUGAN

The basis of Life is love – we would have died out a long time ago if it weren't. Humanity's struggles are based on illusion – things we've made up and chosen to believe about ourselves and others. When those thoughts fall away, there are no problems, only solutions, and we see Life as it really is.

~ What beauty do you see when you drop thinking?

Love is trust.

Trust in love.

LIBBY MCGUGAN

When you remember that love is

the fabric of everything and that *it is*

intelligent, it's easy to trust. The easiest

way to flow with Life is to trust it.

~ What will you trust life with today?

The power of love

Silent, vast, immeasurable,

Breathing us,

Moving us,

Living us,

Orchestrating all that is.

Unchanging stillness within.

Infinitely kind,

Infinitely loving,

Infinitely giving.

Infinitely patient

Outside of Time.

Asking nothing in return.

~ It's too big for our minds, so don't go there.

The door to love opens

With surrender, not control.

Like the wave

Blending into the ocean,

Realising the power

That dances it to life.

Surrender is one of the most powerful agents of change. When we let go of trying to make things happen the way we think they should, we give the Universe space to work its magic. The Universe loves space. Don't cramp its style by insisting on particular outcomes – let it surprise and delight you.

~ **What thoughts will you surrender today?**

Soften your awareness

From thinking

To focusing.

From trying to control details,

To the feeling – tone of what you prefer...

Love? Harmony? Peace? Joy?

Set the tone for your day

And watch the details arrange themselves

Like magic.

Your power is limitless but it is subtle. It has no
need to force but you have to tune to it to work
with it. It is the frequency you choose to radiate
that shapes the world around you. When you get
this, you become the artist of your life experience.

~ What tone will you set today?

CHAPTER FOUR

SOUL

Our soul is the bridge

Between our mind

And the Mind of Life.

Think of it like a funnel. At the lower tip is our egoic personal thinking and all the problems it innocently creates. As our awareness expands upwards in the funnel, there is more space to grow. The top of the funnel is open-ended... it connects us to everyone and to the intelligence of Life itself. Living at the level of our soul means living at a higher level of consciousness. It's more peaceful, more powerful and way more fun. Like a hot air balloon naturally rises when it drops its weights, our level of consciousness naturally rises when we drop heavy thoughts.

~ What can you drop today to rise up naturally?

As bees need flowers

And plants need sunlight,

We are part of the vast web of Life.

Everyone, everything interconnected,

Our imprints are felt by all.

The energy, the thoughts, the feelings we radiate

Touch everyone.

Growing up is choosing

To radiate wisely.

The energy connecting us is real and our thoughts and actions have a ripple effect on the fabric of the world around us. We have a responsibility to choose our focus carefully – what we focus on comes to life, remember? Every day is an opportunity to consciously radiate positive change.

~ What energy would you prefer to radiate to those you love?

In the majesty of the Cosmos,

I fall silent

And hear my soulsong.

Life created you as you for a reason. No-one else can be you except you. Your soulsong is who you came here to be.

~ Enjoy singing your soulsong to its fullest.

Let your soul

Align your body-mind

To all that you came here to become.

LIBBY MCGUGAN

Your soul doesn't exist inside your body.

Your body and mind exist inside your soul.

~ Relax and let it shape you.

Let go of drama.

Your soul is calling you

To live above the line.

You know when you dip into lower levels of consciousness – life becomes messy, problems (that you innocently make up) multiply and you feel low. Rather than try to sort out all those dramas, put them down and automatically you'll rise to a higher level. Here, solutions are obvious and those problems may not even exist anymore. Life is much simpler than we make it out to be.

~ How is your soul calling you to live?

As the night sky has no walls between stars

And space has no boundary,

Our soul connects us

To everyone

And everything

That is right for our path.

Life's wisdom knows what is right for us – we don't have to figure it out. What's right for us feels good in our core. When we live at the level of our soul, serendipity is natural. We meet the right people at the right time. We know the right things to say. Opportunities open up effortlessly and life's magic unfolds with grace and ease. It's the place to live.

~ What happens when you let Life's wisdom guide you?

The sound of your soulsong

Pure, clear, true

Calls you into alignment.

No need to control the world.

The energy of Life flows through you

And creates your world for you.

When we create from our egos, life is messy, complex and difficult. When we create from our soul, life is magical. We are always creating, but *where we choose to create from* shapes our world. We always have a choice.

~ What do you choose?

What we focus on,

We radiate.

What we radiate,

The world reflects.

We are creators of our experience,

Learning to align

With our soul's truth:

To live our best life.

LIBBY MCGUGAN

There's bad news and good news. The bad news

is that we are responsible for our creations.

The good news is that we are responsible for

our creations! When we *really get that we are*

creators, we can consciously create from a

place of integrity, love and joy for our highest

good and the highest good of all. The world is

our mirror – all we have to do is smile first.

~ What will you create today?

Alignment is a call to create

Love, joy, wisdom, peace

In its infinite expressions.

LIBBY MCGUGAN

The paradox is that you have to give up control
to gain control. You have to let go of who you
think you are to become who you really are.

**~ Let Life celebrate and express
itself through you fully,
with no hesitation.**

Our true desires

Are Life's desires

Born of love, asking to be lived.

Nurture them,

Honour them,

Appreciate them.

Expand with them

And Life's goodness will blossom.

You have your own unique blueprint – your unique set of preferences, perspectives, gifts and skills. Your true desires are simply a means to express your blueprint. You matter because you bring something to the table that Life needs and that no-one else can bring.

~ Let yourself live who you really are.

Thoughts come and go.

People come and go.

The world comes and goes.

Who you are does not come and go.

Unchanging stillness,

Loving, wise awareness,

Creating through intention.

LIBBY MCGUGAN

~ Do you know that you are Divine?

Your soul is the parent

To your mind.

Let it hold you

Let it guide you

Let it be you.

LIBBY MCGUGAN

~ Stop struggling and let Life live you.

It knows what it's doing.

What a joy

To be aware

That we are alive.

Shaped by Love,

Shaping Love,

The fabric of Life's infinite abundance.

LIBBY MCGUGAN

There is nothing more powerful than to wake up to the fact that we are alive and that we are creators. We can create a better world through the power of our focus and the actions that flow through us from wisdom. We have the joy of consciously choosing the kind of world we want to live in.

~ Choose wisely, celebrate Life and watch what happens.

I RECOMMEND

Coming Home: Uncovering the Foundations of Psychological Well-being, Dicken Bettinger and Natasha Swedloff (Createspace Independent Publishing Platform, 2016)

The Power of Now, Eckhart Tolle, (Yellow Kite, 1999)

Ask and It Is Given, Esther and Jerry Hicks (Hay House 2004)

Super Accelerated Living, Bentinho Massaro (Trinfinity Publishing, 2016)

The Zen Way to the Martial Arts, Taisen Deshimaru (Rider, 1983)

Tao Te Ching, An Illustrated Journey, Lao Tzu, translated by Stephen Mitchell (Frances Lincoln Limited, 1999)

I Hope I Screw This Up, Kyle Cease (Gallery Books, 2017)

The Universe Has Your Back, Gabrielle Bernstein (Hay House, 2016)

The Missing Link, Reflections of Philosophy & Spirit, Sydney Banks (Lone Pine Publishing and Partners Publishing, 1998)

Breath of the Absolute, Mooji (Yogi Impressions Books, 2010)

A Course In Miracles, Course in Miracles Society (Course in Miracles Society 2012)

The Universe in a Single Atom, His Holiness the Dalai Lama (Little, Brown, 2005)

Buddhist Boot Camp, Timber Hawkeye (Harper One, 2013)

Light Is The New Black, Rebecca Campbell (Hay House, 2015)

ABOUT THE AUTHOR

Libby McGugan is an author, inspirational speaker and TEDx speaker, mentor and musician. She is passionate about helping people connect with their true nature, the wisdom of their heart and the blueprint of their soul, so that they can live their best lives freely and fully.

Before being called to change careers, she was an emergency medicine consultant and draws on her medical background as a bridge between science and the human spirit. She now guides people to see the miracle of the whole human system and how to work with it to live life fully.

Nominated for Best Newcomer in the British Fantasy Awards for her first novel, *The Eidolon*, she loves pointing people to a deeper understanding of consciousness through metaphysical storytelling. The screenplay of her first book continues to draw interest from several large production companies.

She loves music, seeing it as the closest thing to our true nature, and loves playing the fiddle in the alternative-folk band, Bensider, with her partner, Graham.

Printed and bound by CPI Group (UK) Ltd, Croydon, CR0 4YY